Juliana Rufino Orthmeyer

Knowledge Production on Physical Education Training in Brazil

Juliana Rufino Orthmeyer

Knowledge Production on Physical Education Training in Brazil

ScienciaScripts

Imprint
Any brand names and product names mentioned in this book are subject to trademark, brand or patent protection and are trademarks or registered trademarks of their respective holders. The use of brand names, product names, common names, trade names, product descriptions etc. even without a particular marking in this work is in no way to be construed to mean that such names may be regarded as unrestricted in respect of trademark and brand protection legislation and could thus be used by anyone.

Cover image: www.ingimage.com

This book is a translation from the original published under ISBN 978-3-8417-2573-8.

Publisher:
Sciencia Scripts
is a trademark of
Dodo Books Indian Ocean Ltd. and OmniScriptum S.R.L publishing group

120 High Road, East Finchley, London, N2 9ED, United Kingdom
Str. Armeneasca 28/1, office 1, Chisinau MD-2012, Republic of Moldova, Europe
Printed at: see last page
ISBN: 978-620-8-07987-1

To the workers, may the knowledge historically produced
ensure decent conditions of existence.
Construction

He loved that time as if it were the last He kissed his wife as if it were the last And each of his children as if it were the only one And he crossed the street with his timid step He climbed the building as if it were a machine He erected four solid walls on the landing Brick by brick in a magical design His eyes dulled with cement and tears He sat down to rest as if it were Saturday He ate beans and rice as if he were a prince He drank and sobbed as if he were a castaway He danced and laughed as if he heard music And he stumbled across the sky as if he were a drunk And he floated in the air as if he were a bird And he ended up on the ground like a flaccid package He agonised in the middle of the public pavement He died on the wrong side of the road holding up traffic

Chico Buarque de Holanda, 1971

The premises we started with are not arbitrary, they are not dogmas, they are real premises, and they can only be abstracted from in the imagination. They are real individuals, their actions and their material living conditions, both those they have encountered and those they have produced through their own actions. These premises are therefore purely empirically verifiable (MARX and ENGELS, 2009, p.03 and 04).

The first premise of all human history is naturally the existence of living human individuals. The first presupposition of all human existence is that men must be able to live in order to make history. In order to live, men must, above all, eat, drink, live in and wear clothes. The first historical act is therefore the production of the means to satisfy these needs, the production of material life itself. The truth is that this is a historical act, a fundamental condition of all history, which even today, as thousands of years ago, has to be carried out day by day, hour by hour, to at least keep men alive (MARX and ENGELS, 2009).

In order to produce his existence, man comes into contact with nature and transforms it according to his needs and interests. He transforms himself through work and in this way humanises himself. "One can refer to consciousness, religion and anything else one likes as a distinction between men and animals; however, this distinction only comes into existence when men begin to produce the means of life, a step forward which is the consequence of their bodily organisation" (MARX and ENGELS, 1974, p.19). By producing their means of existence, men indirectly produce their own material life (MARX and ENGELS, 1974).

Human existence is produced through labour. It is possible to state without a shadow of a doubt that training for work has always existed, regardless of the type of work that each individual carries out, and according to the way it is processed in each social formation (slavery, feudalism, capitalism). "[...] man needs to continually produce his own existence. To do this, instead of adapting to nature, he has to adapt nature to himself, that is, transform it. And this is done through labour". (SAVIANI, 2008, p. 11). But what are man's relations with nature? Who performs labour?

> Above all, labour is a process in which man and nature participate, a process in which the human being, through his own action, drives, regulates and controls his material exchange with nature. [...] By acting on external nature and modifying it, he simultaneously modifies his own nature. It develops its dormant potentialities and submits the play of natural forces to its dominion. This is not about instinctive, animal forms

> of labour. When the worker arrives at the market to sell his labour power, the historical distance between his condition and that of primitive man with his still instinctive form of labour is immense. We assume labour in an exclusively human form. A spider carries out operations similar to those of a weaver, and a bee surpasses more than one architect when building its hive. But what distinguishes the worst architect from the best bee is that he figures out his construction in his mind before turning it into reality. [...] He doesn't just transform the material on which he works; he imprints on the material the project he consciously had in mind, which constitutes the determining law of his way of working and to which he has to subordinate his will. (MARX, 2006, p. 211-212).

Through work, man generates and accumulates knowledge so that human history or knowledge is not constantly recreated, the need arises to accumulate and store this knowledge so that progress can be made in human history. So that it doesn't stagnate, so that it doesn't have to start all over again, mankind needs to: (a) store information; (b) pass it on to subsequent generations; and (c) produce new knowledge. In this way, progress is optimised and society does not run the risk of losing its cultural heritage (SAVIANI, 2008, p.11-15). It is therefore necessary to relay and store the knowledge produced. It must be passed on to as many people as possible, because it is this knowledge that enables a better and more dignified production of existence, with greater and fairer opportunities for acquiring culture, art, dance, languages, travelling and so on. In short, all the pleasures and opportunities that work makes possible.

The link between the production of existence - a question of totality - and the production of knowledge - a question of specificity - occurs because of four factors: knowledge as one of the main productive forces of the 21st century favours social, scientific and technological development, as well as art and education (SANTOS JUNIOR, 2005); because of the dialectical relationship between the production of existence and the production of knowledge, in which scientific progress can enable better conditions of existence and vice versa, because the real world is related to the world of ideas; the production of knowledge starts from the way in which existence is produced, and responds to the questions posed by reality. This is because life is not produced from heaven to earth. On the contrary, the movement is from earth to heaven (MARX and ENGELS, 2009); added to the relations of contradiction in which the mastery and appropriation of knowledge justifies and enables social inequalities.

I believe that the production of knowledge can explain the advances and limits of the productive forces and the relations of production, providing critical and punctuated feedback on the reading and exposition of the complexities of the mode of production, in order to open our eyes to the ideology imposed by the owners of the productive forces.

By perpetuating the knowledge it has accumulated, humanity guarantees the progress of more advanced forms of production of existence. This is done in a continuous act of action on nature, until the social division of labour takes place. With the constant specialisation and complexification of work, it is necessary to produce knowledge that makes it possible to advance the productive forces, which enables the production of increasingly complex and elaborate knowledge.

Since the production of knowledge and science seek to resolve questions posed by experience, in other words, the influence that the production of knowledge suffers in the face of the advance of productive forces and vice versa. They also seek to store knowledge so that people don't have to be in a constant state of rediscovery, which implies a lack of cultural heritage and almost no prospect of advancing the productive forces and humanising people.

The movement presented above is characteristic of the Physical Education professional as a *sine qua non* condition for survival. It transforms nature and has human beings as its object of action. Historically, this relationship has been built up on a day-to-day basis, where the production of knowledge has been storing, rethinking and recreating this reality.

In the meantime, the production of knowledge discusses the basis and course of training and explains its relationship with concrete reality. However, there is a lack of elements to truly understand how this process is constituted and what its interferences are. Aware of the importance of knowledge and recognising the production of knowledge in the history of humanity, we cannot lose sight of mapping this production.

With this in mind, I aimed to obtain an overview of the production of knowledge in dissertations and theses on professional training in Physical Education in Brazil, thanks to the structuring of a database of dissertations and theses that subsidised training at postgraduate level in this country.

The specific objectives of this book are to explain the production of knowledge on vocational training in dissertations and theses by means of a survey, cataloguing, compilation and analysis that made it possible to recognise: (1) the flow and volume of production over time in Brazil; (2) the main authors who produce in this area in Brazil, (3) the privileged themes and what motivates production, and (4) the supervisors of these works.

Recognising the state of the art of this production has enabled a more comprehensive view of reality and is of fundamental importance, since it favours the recognition of significant problems that have not yet been studied. In this sense, Saviani (1987) points out that knowledge of the state of the art in a given field of knowledge is essential for its development, since "[...] the unknown is only defined by confrontation with the known, that is, if one does not master what is already known, it is not possible to detect what is not yet known, in order to incorporate it, through research, into the domain of what is already known" (SAVIANI, 1987, p. 51).

This study is justified by the fact that knowledge has been used more than at any time in human history as a productive force (SANTOS JUNIOR, 2005). Thus, I made an effort to look at relations from a dialectical perspective of the capitalist mode of production in order to recognise the links, contradictions and stage of development of this productive force in Brazilian Physical Education. Denying these relationships leads to a fragmented view and does not help in understanding reality. Silva (1991, p. 223) points out that "Knowledge has been incorporated by capital as a productive force, as well as being developed and manipulated as one of its main elements in the process of valorisation and accumulation [...]". Taffarel (1993, p. 91) corroborates this by pointing out that the production of knowledge enables greater accumulation of wealth, in which "Science and technology are recognised as productive forces, because their incorporation into the production process increases labour productivity, produces surplus value, ensuring the accumulation of capital and the conditions that perpetuate it."

I consider this production to be very valuable, recalling Marx (1974) who points out that within the framework of the Materialist and Dialectical Conception of History, it is made explicit that the productive forces are subordinated to the dominant forces of the social relations of production. In the current mode of production, the productive forces as a whole are subordinated to the interests of the bourgeoisie, recognised today as market interests. I consider the discussion about the processes of controlling the production of knowledge to be essential for unveiling the processes of controlling the development of the productive forces undertaken by capitalism.

Chapter 1

The methodological journey

In this research, in the survey stage, I aimed to structure a database of dissertations and theses so that it would be an important tool for Brazilian postgraduate programmes.

To carry out this study, I used bibliographical research. According to Severino (2007, p. 122), bibliographical research "is that which is carried out on the basis of the available record, resulting from previous research, in printed documents, such as books, articles, theses etc". For this research, I used as a basis the study developed by Peixoto (2007) in her doctoral thesis entitled *Estudos do lazer no Brasil: apropriação das obras de Marx e Engels (Leisure studies in Brazil: appropriation of the works of Marx and Engels)*, in which the author produced an exhaustive synthesis of the debate in the field of leisure studies, ranging from organising the flow of production by year, locating the period of production of the first works and transformations throughout history to explaining the production in the light of Marxism and the historical reasons that led to that production.

The survey of the production of knowledge on training was carried out on the basis of the CVs registered on the Lattes Platform, located in a search by subject, using the filter *doctors*, using the exact phrases, *training of physical education teachers* and *training of physical education professionals*.

After this, I accessed each of the researchers' CVs and found and searched the titles of the dissertations and theses[1] for the keywords *training* and *Physical Education*, and the papers that had these two descriptors were part of the *corpus*.

In the survey process I located and catalogued 88 theses and dissertations, and in this search I found 88 researchers. Of these, 53 discussed the topic of "Physical Education teacher training" and 27 discussed the topic of "Physical Education professional training" and 8 discussed both. Of the 88 works catalogued, 32 are theses and 56 are dissertations.

After surveying the curricula, selecting, cataloguing and classifying the works according to the type of press, I analysed the predominant themes. These were located by analysing the titles of the 88 works. The themes - presented in alphabetical order - along with the number of works were:

---

[1] According to productivity categories defined by the CNPq and adopted by the Lattes Platform, *Production in C,T & A,* bibliographic production. Available at: http://lattes.cnpq.br/ Accessed on: 09/03/2009 17h42'.

assessment (11); curriculum (9); history (7); intervention (5); policies (8); training processes (19); knowledge production (12); regulation (1) and knowledge and competences (15); theories, conceptions and methodologies (1). The localisation of these themes allowed the papers to be classified.

These 88 selected dissertations and theses were catalogued in an *Access* database (2003), taking into account firstly the complete references of the works and secondly the specific information regarding the year, author, title, sub-theme, type (theses, dissertations) which made it possible to organise graphs representing the volume of production according to each of the parameters scored.

After the survey and cataloguing, I analysed the dissertations and theses based on the following parameters: (a) the approximate proportion of works dedicated to the discussion of training; (b) the historical period in which the production of dissertations and theses on training in Physical Education took place; (c) the authors who produced them and (d) the most privileged themes.

Analysing the production of dissertations and theses

With the aim of finding out about the stage of development of knowledge production in dissertations and theses on professional training in Physical Education, this chapter has carried out the task of presenting empirical data on: (1) the flow and volume of this production over time in order to find out when it began to take place in Brazil; (2) the main authors who are producing in this area in Brazil, (3) the themes favoured and (4) the supervisors found.

Volume and flow of production in Dissertations and Theses

As described in Chapter 2, the survey of knowledge production in dissertations and theses relating to studies on Physical Education training in Brazil was organised in an electronic database. This decision made it possible to visualise the flow and volume of this production, identifying the period in which it began and the amount of production per year. Let's see:

Table 01: Flow of knowledge production in Dissertations and Theses on Physical Education training in Brazil from 1992 to 1999.

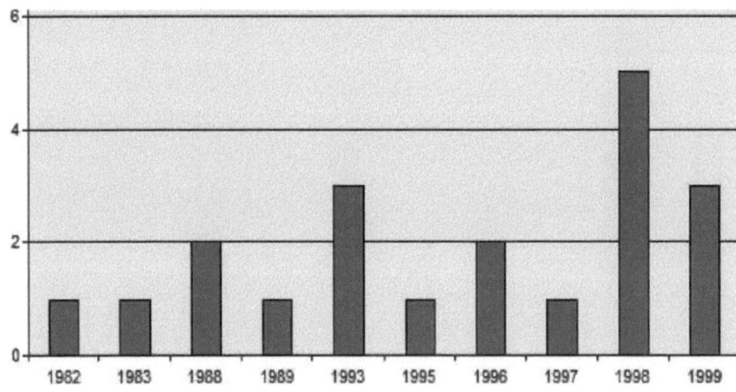

Source: data organised in this book.

The production of knowledge began in 1982 with one paper, and remained constant in 1983. There were no publications in 1984, 1985, 1986, 1987, 1990, 1991, 1992 and 1994. In 1988, 1996 and 2004 there were 2 papers. In 1993 I found 3 works, while in 1995 production fell to 1 work, the following year it increased to 2 works, but the following year it fell again to 1 work. In 1998 there were 5 works and the following year only 3.

The data from 2000 to 2010 is shown in the table below:

Table 02: Flow of knowledge production in Dissertations and Theses on Physical Education training in Brazil from 2000 to 2010.

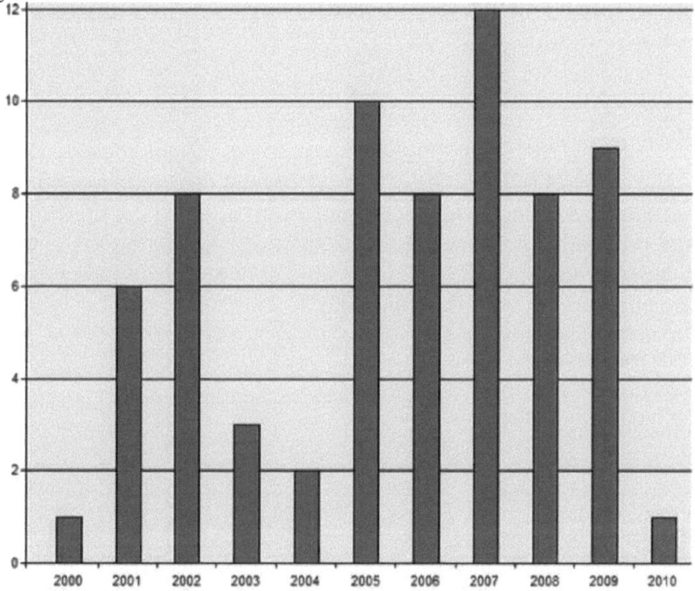

Source: data organised in this book.

After falling in 1998, production only recovered in 2001. Then there was another drop, but in 2005 production increased sharply to 10 works. In 2006, 8 works were produced. 2007 was the most productive year with 12 works, but the following year there was a reduction, totalling 8 works. In 2009 there was a slight increase to 9 works, certainly due to the increase in postgraduate programmes and greater incentives from funding bodies.

Although production began in the 1980s, it reached a reasonable level in the 2000s with an average of eight papers a year. This identifies a fairly recent and inconstant production in the country.

Of the works found, a large proportion focused on the training of PE teachers (53 works), a smaller proportion on the training of PE professionals (27 works), and finally, a total of 8 works did not make it clear whether they were talking about teachers or professionals. The data shows a major gap in the production of knowledge about professionals. The field of Education has certainly contributed to this greater production.

- Themes

The analysis of the titles of the catalogued dissertations and theses (on professional training in Physical Education) allowed me to identify the following predominant themes in the production: According to the volume of knowledge production shown in the table above, the following themes were prioritised along with the following

Table 03: Volume of production on assessment, curriculum, history, intervention and policies. **Source:** data organised in this book.

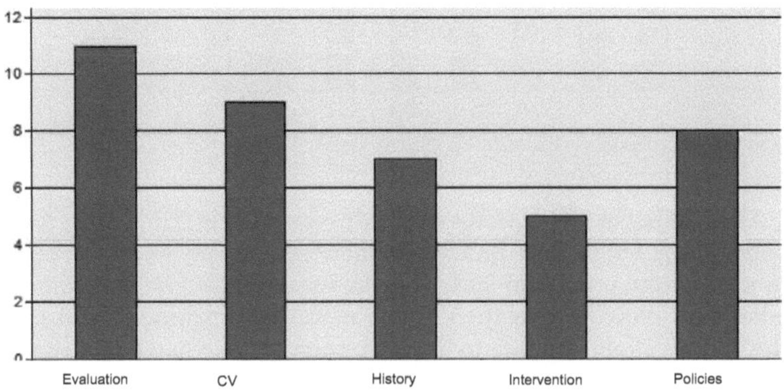

number of papers: assessment (11); curriculum (9); history (7); intervention (5); policies (8).

In the following table I present other themes identified:

Table 04: Volume of production on training processes, knowledge production, regulation, knowledge and competences, and theories, concepts and methodologies.

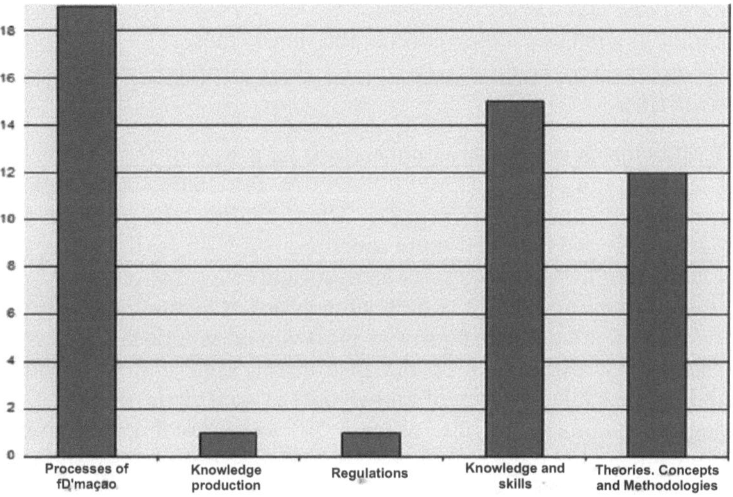

According to the volume, the following themes were prioritised in the production of knowledge - accompanied by the number of papers: training processes (19); knowledge production (1); regulation (1); knowledge and competences (15); theories, conceptions and methodologies (12).

I would emphasise that the number of studies on *regulation* and the *production of knowledge* is very low, which reinforces our premise that much is produced on vocational training, but little is studied about this production, its directions, objectives and theoretical references.

On the contrary, many researchers have been investigating the themes of *training processes*; *knowledge and competences*; *theories, conceptions and methodologies*. These are more technical aspects of education and teaching. This information is corroborated in the work of COSTA (*et al.*, 2010) in which the authors analysed all the productions made at the Brazilian College of Sports Sciences on professional training and identified that the themes most evident among the selected articles were: *curriculum*; *knowledge and skills for training*; and *social representations*.

Below is a detailed description of the sub-themes.

A - Evaluation

Evaluation in education is understood as a way of monitoring the teaching-learning process, seeking to identify difficulties and gaps in learning in order to favour this process. These studies take place on two levels, one broader and the other more specific.

On the first level, thanks to an analysis and investigation of learning in these dissertations and theses, which were aimed at learning about broad professional training and, consequently, professional practice. The second has the same objective, but it is the instrument itself that is aimed at understanding the students' stage of knowledge, as well as the possibility of monitoring development in the process of understanding, critiquing, assimilating and applying the knowledge learnt during professional training.

Eleven papers focused on Physical Education and discussed: (1) professional training and citizenship in the teaching of Physical Education at university level; (2) initial training on the way to teachers' pedagogical practice; (3) undergraduate and bachelor's degree courses and their proposals for professional training, as well as the theoretical and practical implications; (4) school Physical Education as a process in the training of students; (5) professional training and the teaching of assessment; (6) the contributions of the PPGs.

(7) metamorphoses in Physical Education assessment: from initial training to school pedagogical practice; (8) the Florianópolis School of Physical Education and the field of teacher training in the state of Santa Catarina: a history, a look, an identity; (9) teacher training in Brazil: advances and setbacks; (10) the subject of recreation and leisure in the professional training curriculum: what teachers say and do at universities in the north-east of Brazil; (11) the meanings of professional training in the imagination of undergraduate teachers at UFAL.

B - CV

Nine papers were discussed: (1) folklore and popular culture in the training of professionals, senses and meanings of Carnival; (2) the clash of training projects and the duality of degree and bachelor's degree; (3) professional preparation in Physical Education and the issue of internships; (4) teacher training at UEL and the translation of the curriculum project by teachers; (5) transformation of initial teacher training and the curriculum internship and internship issues; (6) the subject of basketball and teacher training; (7) pedagogical innovations in the curriculum of professional training courses and theoretical-methodological contributions; (8) the creative chain in the training of educators based on the curricular proposal of the State of São Paulo for the subject of Physical Education; (9) gymnastics as an area of knowledge in professional training and the guidelines for structuring the curriculum.

According to the data I found, I observed that researchers who study this subject devote a lot of time to discussing the subjects that make up the curriculum, internships, training projects, fragmented training and theoretical-methodological contributions.

C - History

The fact that there are only 7 papers produced is worrying, given that mastering history is essential because: "History is not an end in itself. It helps us understand the present and plan for the future [...]" (FRANCO, 2002, p. 119). It is an important tool for reading reality and possibly transforming it in any area of knowledge and historical moment. During their undergraduate studies, students come into contact with the history of Brazilian and world physical education; however, they have almost no contact with the content of the history of education or with Brazilian and world history, creating a gap in their education.

Seven papers discussed the following themes: (1) science and professional training; (2) the reorganisation of professional training in Physical Education in Brazil and its significant historical aspects; (3) human motricity in the history of UNICAMP; (4) the labour market *versus* emancipatory historical possibilities; (5) memory, sport and teacher training; (6) the subject of History of Physical Education in initial training; (7) the history of Physical Education in Bahia and the path of professional training.

D - Intervention

The intervention sub-theme included studies that sought to address professional practice in the school and professional fields. Five papers discussed: (1) the occupation of the Physical Education labour market in Campinas; (2) graduation and its reflexes in the cities of Santo André, São Bernardo and São Caetano do Sul; (3) the contribution of teaching practice in teacher training; (4) the relationship between the pedagogical intention and action of higher education teachers and (5) dance in the context of training and professional performance.

E - Policies

Eight papers discussed: (1) new legal frameworks and assumptions for a new pedagogy of results; (2) the Centre for Physical Education and Sport at the Federal University of Bahia as a popular reference centre for teacher training and body culture: the reality and possibilities of a public space; (3) continuous teacher training in São Paulo and the policies at stake; (4) the liberal trend in professional training; (5) an analysis of the legal relationships that guide training and the national plans in Brazilian Education and Sport; (6) teacher training and its relationship with the world of life; (7) a study on political training and, (8) teaching and training for citizenship in secondary education.

Considering that mastery of the policies at play in vocational training are key elements for improving the professional class in terms of working conditions and remuneration, we see that this category is being little studied, given that the obstacles and difficulties are enormous. It is therefore pertinent to question the low level of interest in this subject of study according to the data found.

Costa (*et all*, 2010) points out that among the themes favoured by researchers who have studied Physical Education training, little has been discussed about it in settlements, rural and indigenous communities and the work of lay teachers. When I asked myself why this was not the case, I realised that there is no interest in preparing these minority groups because they have minimal access to the production of elaborate knowledge.

There is no interest in these groups reaching more elaborate levels of thought and knowledge. On the contrary, it's in their interest to remain isolated and alienated from development and technology. For the liberal government is not interested in minorities, especially those who are opposed to government policies, such as the landless, homeless and indigenous communities. It is interested in destabilising groups that have a communist, socialist or anarchist worldview and thus repudiating movements that go against the system.

F - Training Processes

In 19 papers I found the following themes: (1) multicultural teacher training; (2) teacher training and professional development for educational innovation; (3) pedagogical practice of primary school teachers and the contributions of initial and continuing training; (4) *cyberculture* and the virtual world in teacher training; (5) Physical Education and constructivism in the search for a path in continuing teacher training; (6) school physical education in Goiás and continuing teacher training: realities and perspectives; (7) panorama and perspective of/for continuing education and the paths of *lato sensu* post-graduation in Bahia; (8) social experiences in the process of teacher education; (9) network of participated self-education as a form of professional development; (10) permanent teacher education in the municipal education network of Porto Alegre in the period from 1989 to 1999; (11) action-research and the insertion of the media in continuing teacher education; (12) continuing education in the municipal education network of Santa Maria; (13) ongoing training and its relationship with teacher practice in Porto Alegre's municipal sports, recreation and leisure department; (14) ongoing training for nursery school teachers and the lesson diary technique; (15) ongoing teacher training and their reflective practices; (16) initial training and a critical and reflective experience in inclusive physical education; (17) continuing training and the reflections and challenges of primary school teachers; (18) continuing training for early childhood education teachers in Florianópolis from 1993 to 2004; and continuing training for teachers in an inclusive school environment.

The topic of *continuing education* is the most studied by researchers, and is an important tool for teachers to acquire more knowledge and have greater autonomy in their positions and decision-making processes. This process depends on several factors, so we must break with the common sense idea disseminated by the media that blames the teacher as being solely responsible for their training and intervention, disregarding a series of empirical data.

This process will be relevant if it enables the teacher to have contact with colleagues in the field, trained teachers, access to up-to-date literature and access to politicised knowledge, participating in revolutionary movements and with in-depth knowledge of the reality of professional intervention.

However, the process of continuing training is surrounded by limitations, so we must see its real potential for collaboration, without expecting it to solve the problems of professional practice, which are many and diverse.

G - Knowledge Production

I only found one dissertation that discussed trends in professional training in undergraduate Physical Education, written by Adriana Machado Penna, produced at the Fluminense Federal University in the Master's programme in Education in 2006.

In view of the great concern for greater knowledge production, an important criterion established and demanded by CAPES, I hypothesised that the number of productions on this topic would be relevant. However, it wasn't, which means that production takes place without being analysed or evaluated.

It is produced without direction, without knowledge of the objects and gaps found. This data strengthens the intention of this study, to explain the production of knowledge on Physical Education training in Brazil.

H - Regulation

I only found one paper that discussed the CONFEF/CREFS system as an expression of the dominant project of human formation in Physical Education. I would point out that this study included professors with a doctorate, excluding specialists and masters.

However, since the turbulent establishment of CONFEF in 1998, studies on this subject have increased and we currently have a large production thanks mainly to the National Movement Against the Regulation of Physical Education, led by Hajime Nozaki, a national reference in the field.

I noticed that the work produced on the subject of *knowledge production* and *regulation* was written at the Fluminense Federal University in the Postgraduate Programme in Education. This institution appears to be a space made up of teachers and students capable of seeing the gaps in Physical Education. Both were guided by the Marxist framework, which focuses on critical positioning in the face of reality. This leads us to the premise that although there are few Marxists working in Higher Education Institutions within Physical Education, they are reading reality.

I - Knowledge and Skills

In the set of 15 papers, I identified the following objects: (1) intellectual skills and abilities required in teacher training and uncritical training; (2) training guided by the Ecological Systems Theory; (3) characteristics, indicators and importance of creativity and motor creativity in training; (4) academic training and the content of dance; (5) the subject of Artistic Gymnastics in graduate training from the perspective of university teachers; (6) professional training in the context of adventure physical activities in nature; (7) proposal for affectivity and pedagogical practice in a teacher training course; (8) perceived environment and self-perception of professional competence of Brazilian and Portuguese graduates; (9) the subject of leisure and recreation in teacher training: a study on some curricular dealings in Paraná State Universities; (10) the game as knowledge in initial training; (11) the construction of pedagogical competences through practice as a curricular component in initial training; (12) continuing professional training and its contribution to intervention in the health area; (13) contributions of Physical Education as pedagogical practice in the training of autonomous subjects; (14) teacher training, the pedagogical work process and dealing with knowledge; and (15) musical elements to be addressed in training.

Little is invested in the production of knowledge about the skills and competences needed to train and work as a Physical Education professional, and much of this production is not presented to teachers, and when it is, sometimes the language is so complex and distant from professional practice that it is difficult for most to understand. This reality makes it very difficult to master what is known and to transform professional and social intervention.

J - Theories, concepts and methodologies

This set includes 12 works dealing with: (1) swimming teacher training and the contributions of Wallonian principles and concepts; (2) childhood in university teacher training and the emergence of a discipline; (3) adapted Physical Education and a proposal for methodological action for university training; (4) the use of information and communication technologies in Physical Education and Sport teacher training; (5) teacher training and theoretical and methodological mediation; (6) the conceptions of professional training for undergraduates, teaching trajectories and their contributory perspectives; (7) conceptions and the place of Physical Education in the training of secondary school workers; (8) proposals for teaching practice in teacher training; (9) the question of academic training from the point of view of its agents in training; (10) political-pedagogical project, curriculum guidelines and the epistemological clash in initial training in Physical Education; (11) study of professional training proposals; (12) learning theories and their reconstruction in teacher training.

Studying and deepening our knowledge of the technical aspects of education, thinking strictly of the teacher, is of great importance in the sense that each teacher in their school, neighbourhood or city can contribute to better education. However, sticking to these technical aspects won't solve the educational crisis; we need to go further, and that includes time and dedication to read, reflect, discuss and rebuild. Most teachers are not in a position to do this, which is why courses and reading sometimes don't offer significant progress. I agree with Krug when he observed that during the action research carried out with the teachers taking part in his study, they were at the technical level and were unable to move beyond it, failing to reach the practical and critical or emancipatory levels (KRUG, 2004).

Finally, I found that the following themes - policies, training processes, and theories, conceptions and methodologies - were produced at a medium level, 16, 34 and 26 respectively. The themes of history, intervention, production of knowledge and regulation were the least addressed, 11, 11, 9 and 1 respectively.

11.3 - As for the authors and works located

At this point, I will present the works published between the 1980s and 1990s, and the presentation criterion used is chronological, with the aim of drawing up a profile of the production in these decades. The first work located, published in 1982, was the dissertation by CARMO, A. A., entitled *Educação Física, crítica a uma formação acrítica: um estudo das habilidades e capacidades intelectuais solicitadas na formação do professor de Educação Física*, produced by UFSCAR.

The second work located, published in 1983, was the dissertation by SILVA, J. B., entitled *Analyses of the relationships existing in the legislation that guides the professional training of specialists in Physical Education and Sports and the national plans in the educational and sports areas in Brazil*, published by USP.

In 1988, I found two works. Both were dissertations; the first was written by PINTO, V. M. R. R. and was entitled *A tendência liberal na formação do profissional de Educação Física,* produced by UFRJ. The second, written by CARDOSO, Carlos Luiz, was entitled *A proposal for teaching practice in the training of physical education teachers,* produced by UFSM.

In 1989, I found a dissertation written by OLIVEIRA, Iara Regina Damiani; entitled *A Educação Física escolar como processo na formação do educando*, produced by UFSM.

To summarise, in the 1980s we can see that researchers were interested in discussing issues relating to critical training, the legislation that guides training, teaching practice, competences for professional practice, the liberal trend in professional training and school physical education.

Costa (*et all*, 2010 cited by Silva, 2001) points out that Faria Júnior (1980), Cantarino Filho (1986) and Canfield (1985) were concerned with emphasising critical, theoretical-philosophical and epistemological reflection in the field. Of these, only Cantarino Filho is missing from my database.

In 1993, I found three papers, two of which were theses; the first was written by TAFFAREL, C. N. Z., and was entitled *The formation of the education professional: the pedagogical work process and dealing with knowledge in the Physical Education course* produced at UNICAMP. The second was written by TOJAL, J. B. A., and is entitled *A Emergência da motricidade humana no percurso histórico da UNICAMP e bacharelado em Educação Física* - mercado de trabalho e formação profissional produced at UTL in Lisbon. The third work is the dissertation by VALENTE, M. C. entitled *A disciplina recreação e lazer no currículo de formação de profissionais de Educação Física:* o que dizem e fazem professores em universidades do Nordeste do Brasil produced at UNICAMP.

In 1995, a dissertation was written by RESENDE, H. G., entitled *Relação entre a intenção e a ação pedagógica de professores atuantes no processo de formação de futuros professores de Educação Física (Relationship between the intention and the pedagogical action of teachers in the training process of future Physical Education teachers)*, published at UERJ.

In 1996 I found 2 dissertations; the first was written by ROMBALDI, Rosiane de Magalhães and was entitled *A formação profissional em Educação Física e o ensino da avaliação (Professional training in Physical Education and the teaching of assessment)*, produced at UFSM. The second was written by OLIVEIRA, M. J. A. S., and is entitled *Folklore and Popular Culture in the Training of Physical Education Professionals:* Senses and Meanings of Carnival, produced at Gama Filho.

In 1997 I found a thesis in Education, written by VIEIRA, Péricles Saremba, entitled *Professional training and citizenship in the teaching of Physical Education at* university *level,* produced at UFSCAR.

In 1998 I found 5 works, 3 of which were dissertations. The first was written by WURDIG, Rogério Costa, and was entitled *From university benches to schoolyards*: from initial training to the pedagogical practice of physical education teachers, and was produced at UFSC. The second dissertation was written by MORENO, José Carlos de Almeida, and is entitled *A disciplina basquetebol e a formação de professores de Educação Física,* produced at Unicamp. The third dissertation was written by ANDERÁOS, M., and is entitled *Estudo das propostas de formação profissional desenvolvidas pela Faculdade de Educação Física de Santo André,* also produced at Unicamp. The first thesis found was by SIMÕES, R. M. R., and is entitled *From the body in time to the time of the body:* Science and Professional Training in Physical Education, also produced at Unicamp. The second thesis found was written by NASCIMENTO, Juarez Vieira and is entitled *A formação inicial universitária em educação física e desportos:* uma abordagem sobre o ambiente percebido e autopercepção de competência profissional de graduantes brasileiros e portugueses, produced at the University of Porto.

In 1999 I found 3 works; a thesis and a dissertation produced at Unicamp, as follows: the first was written by VALENTE, M. C., entitled *A formação profissional* em *Educação Física & Esporte:* mercado de trabalho x possibilidades históricas emancipatórias. The second was written by DELGADO, M. A., entitled *Occupation of the Physical Education Labour Market in the City of Campinas due to Professional Training.* The last work is a thesis written by SOUZA NETO, Samuel, entitled *Physical Education at University:* Licenciatura and Bacharelado - the Proposals for Professional Training and their Theoretical-Practical Implications, produced at USP.

The early 1990s were marked by productions on pedagogical work, dealing with knowledge, recreation and leisure subjects in the training curriculum, human motricity at Unicamp, the relationship between undergraduates' pedagogical intentions and actions, assessment in training, folklore and popular culture, citizenship in the Physical Education course, training and intervention in Physical Education, science and professional training, self-perception of competence, basketball in training, training proposals in Santo André, occupation of the labour market, disintegrated training and emancipatory historical possibilities in the labour market.

In this period, the production of knowledge geared towards market interests (mainly publishing) predominated, as far as professional training was concerned (PEIXOTO, 2007). There was great concern about bureaucratised knowledge production and its quantity over the quality of the work.

11.4 - Regarding the area of production in Dissertations and Theses

As for the production of dissertations and theses by area of production (Education and/or Physical Education), we have the following scenario:

Table 01: Volume of dissertations and theses according to area of production.

HEI	Physical Education		Education		Total works
	D	T	D	T	
PUCSP	0	0	0	4	1
UERJ	5	0	1	0	1
UFBA	5	0	3	2	5
UFF	0	0	0	2	2
UFMG	0	0	1	0	1
UFSC	12	0	2	0	19
UFSCAR	0	0	2	0	2
UFSM	2	2	5.	0	2
UFPE	5	0	2	2	3.
LJFRGS	3	0	0	2	1
UFRJ	0	0	2	1	3
UGF	1	1	0	0	2
UNICAMP	2	2	0	5	23
UNESPRC	3	0	0	0	3
LJP	1	0	0	0	1
USP	2	0	1	1	4
UTL	1	0	1	0	2
TOTAL	34	12	25	17	88

Source: data found in this study.

Of all the dissertations and theses found in higher education institutions, UNICAMP is the most productive with a total of 23 works. UNICAMP is a reference for the study of professional training in Physical Education in Brazil, both in the training of researchers who study this subject and the consumers of these works. This is followed by UFSC with 19 works; UFSM with 09 works; UFBA with 5 works; USP, PUCSP and UFRGS with 4 works each; UFRJ, UFPE and UNESP/RC with 3 works each.

Among the Postgraduate Programmes, Physical Education produced fewer theses (12) than Education (17). This is due to the scarcity of doctoral programmes. In terms of dissertations, the opposite is true: Physical Education produced 34 dissertations while Education produced 25.

At UNICAMP there were 9 theses and 9 dissertations in the Physical Education programme, while in Education there were no dissertations, but a significant number of theses (5). No theses were produced at UFSC. Of the dissertations written, 12 are from the Physical Education programme and the rest from Education. At UFSM, 2 theses were produced in Physical Education. More dissertations were produced in the Education programme (5) than in Physical Education (2). At UFBA, production is in the area of Education, where Celi Taffarel is a reference on Physical Education training in Brazil. Three dissertations and two theses were written. At USP, within Physical Education, I found 2 dissertations. In Education, 1 thesis and 1 dissertation. At PUC-SP I found 4 theses in the field of Education. UFRGS produced 3 dissertations in Physical Education and only 1 thesis in Education. At UFRJ and UFPE, studies were concentrated in Education, with 2 dissertations and 1 thesis. At UNESP/RC there were 3 dissertations in the area of Physical Education.

11.5 - As for the supervisors of the dissertations and theses

Below, I present, in order of greatest production, the supervisors of the 88 dissertations and theses surveyed, with the total and type of work they supervised.

Table 02: Supervisors and total number of works supervised.

Advisor	Number of T and D orientated	Total orientations
TOJAL, João Batista Andreotti Gomes	*3 Theses and 4 Dissertations*	*7*
NASCIMENTO, Juarez Vieira do	*5 Dissertations*	*5*
KRUG, Hugo Norberto	*4 Dissertations*	*4*
GALLARDO, Jorge Sergio Pérez	2 Theses and 2 dissertations	4
NETO, Vicente Molina	3 Dissertations	3
VAZ, Alexandre Fernandez	2 Dissertations	2
FREITAS, Luiz Carlos de	2 Theses	2
HUNGER, Dagmar	2 Dissertation	2
MAHONEY, Abigail Alvarenga	2 Theses	2
KUNZ, Elenor	2 Dissertations	2
LEIRO, Augusto Cesar Rios	2 Dissertations	2
SHIGUNOV, Viktor	2 Dissertations	2
MOREIRA, Evando Carlos	*Dissertation*	*1*

NETO, Samuel de Souza	*Dissertation*	*1*
TAFFAREL, Celi Neuza zulke	*Thesis*	*1*
ABIB, Pedro Rodolpho Junger	Dissertation	1
ANDRADE, Carmen Maria	Thesis	1
ARAGÃO, Rosalia Ribeiro de	Dissertation	1
ARAÚJO, Clarissa Martins de	Dissertation	1
ASSIS, Orly Zucatto Mantovani de	Thesis	1
BENTO, Jorge Olimpio	Thesis	1
BIANCHETTI, Lucídio	Dissertation	1
BOAVENTURA, Edivaldo Machado	Thesis	1
BORDAS, Mérion Campos	Thesis	1
BOTOMÉ, Sílvio Paulo	Thesis	1
BRITO, Dyla Tavares de Sá	Thesis	1
BUENO, Belmira Amélia de Barros Oliveira	Thesis	1
CANEN, Ana	Dissertation	1
CANFIELD, Marta de Salles	Dissertation	1
CASTELLANI FILHO, Lino	Dissertation	1
CAVALCANTI, Kátia Brandão.	Dissertation	1
COSTA, Vera Lucia de Menezes	Dissertation	1
DAROS, Maria das Dores	Dissertation	1
DINIZ, José Alves	Thesis	1
DUARTE, Edison	Thesis	1
FARIA JUNIOR, Alfredo Gomes de	Dissertation	1
FERRAZ, Osvaldo Luiz	Dissertation	1
FERREIRA, Julio Romero	Thesis	1
FERREIRA, Nilda Teves	Thesis	1
FRANÇA, Tereza Luiza de	Dissertation	1
FRANCO, Maria Laura Puglisi Barbosa	Thesis	1
KREBS, Ruy Jornada	Thesis	1
GAMBOA, Silvio Ancízar Sanchéz	Thesis	1
GARCIA, Maria Beatriz Gorski	Dissertation	1
GOERGEN, Pedro L;	Dissertation	1
MOREIRA, Wagner Wey	Thesis	1
LIBERALI, Fernando Coelho	Dissertation	1
NEIRA, Marcos Garcia	Dissertation	1
PEREIRA, Elisabete Monteiro Aguiar	Thesis	1
PIRES, Giovani De	Dissertation	1
QUINTEIRO, Jucirema	Dissertation	1
REALI, Aline Maria de Medeiros Rodrigues	Thesis	1
REIS, Ronaldo Rosas	Dissertation	1
SANTIAGO, Maria Eliete	Thesis	1
SANTIN, Silvino	Dissertation	1
SILVA, Maurício Roberto da	Dissertation	1

SOUSA, Mário Nunes de	Dissertation	1
SOUZA, Elizabeth Paoliello Machado	Thesis	1
SANTOS, Lucíola Licínio de Castro Paixão	Thesis	1
TREIN, Eunice	Dissertation	1
VALLE, Ione Ribeiro	Dissertation	1
SILVA, Ana Márcia	Dissertation	1
VIEIRA e CUNHA, Manuel Sérgio	Thesis	1
WINTERSTEIN, Pedro José	Dissertation	1

Source: Lattes Platform, IBICT and PPG.

The table above shows Tojal as the most productive supervisor with 7 works (3 theses and 4 dissertations), followed by Nascimento with 5 dissertations; Gallardo (2 theses and 2 dissertations); Krug with 4 dissertations and Neto with 3 dissertations. With the exception of Gallardo, the other four supervisors had their works selected for analysis, which means that they wrote their theses on professional training in Physical Education in Brazil and supervise students in Postgraduate Programmes. This means that they are seen as references, opinion formers who propagate their theoretical framework and their conception of professional training.

Freitas, Hunger, Kunz, Leiro, Mahoney, Shigunov and Vaz appear with 2 orientations. It is pertinent to know the worldview of these authors and their advisees, who are university professors responsible for producing knowledge about training. Next, I presented the supervisors of the Postgraduate Programmes, along with their place of work, level of training and the concept of the programmes in which they work:

Chart 03: Place of work and level of performance in Postgraduate Programmes.

Name	Workplace	Level of performance in postgraduate studies	Programme Score
João Batista G. A. Tojal	UNICAMP	Masters and Doctorates	4
Celi Nelza Z. Taffarel	UFBA	Masters and Doctorates	4
Juarez V. Nascimento	UFSC	Masters and doctorates	5
Samuel de Souza Neto	UNESP/RC	Masters and Doctorates	5

Source: data found in this study.

In a forthcoming study I intend to analyse the works of João Batista Andreotti Gomes Tojal, Celi Nelza Zulke Taffarel, Samuel de Souza Neto and Hugo Norberto Krug. The intended expositions will consider: (a) the physical and structural description (pre-textual, textual and post-textual elements); (b) the justifications presented by the authors for the need to study, research and work in the area of training in education, as well as the historical context that explains their production. In other words, it tries to capture the relevance of the authors' investment in research into vocational training.

Chapter 3

A context that explains and justifies production on training

This stage helped me to understand the context in which the production is immersed and will help the reader to understand from which reference point I start and what I share as truth. I began the literature review by discussing the ontology and centrality of labour, since: "[...] labour can be considered the original phenomenon, the model of social being; it therefore seems methodologically advantageous to begin the analysis of labour, since the clarification of its determinations will result in a precise picture of the essential elements of social being" (LUKÁCS, 1986, p. 10).

Links between Labour and Education

> The act of acting on nature by transforming it to meet human needs is what we know as labour. We can therefore say that the essence of man is labour. The human essence, then, is not given to man; it is not a divine or natural gift; it is not something that precedes man's existence. On the contrary, the human essence is produced by men themselves. What man is, he is through labour. The essence of man is a human achievement. It is a labour that develops, deepens and complexifies over time: it is a historical process (SAVIANI, 2007, p.154).

But what is labour? Labour is the ability to transform nature based on a teleology that aims to adapt it to the interests and needs of man. Such is the importance of labour that it is used to identify and differentiate humans from animals. It is a vital factor for man:

> A spider carries out operations similar to those of a weaver, and a bee surpasses more than one architect when building its hive. But what distinguishes the worst architect from the best bee is that he figures out his construction in his mind before turning it into reality. At the end of the labour process, a result appears that already existed ideally in the worker's imagination (MARX, 2003, p. 211-212).

According to Ávila (2008), Marx points out that animals have their behaviour conditioned by their environment and the instincts of their species. Human beings, on the other hand, are capable of transforming their environment in order to adapt it to meet their needs. The ability to project an idea before it is executed is a human characteristic. Only man possesses this power of abstraction. In this way, man works and is able to transform his environment according to his needs. But labour is more than that, because "it is the source of all wealth," say economists. It is, in fact, the source of all wealth, say economists, alongside nature, which is responsible for providing the materials that it converts into wealth. But labour is much more than that" (MARX, 2006, p. 1). It is the basic and fundamental condition of all human existence and, to a certain extent, we can say that labour created man himself. Several hundred thousand years ago, at a time, not yet definitively established, in that period of the Earth's development that geologists call the Tertiary, probably towards the end of that period, "there lived somewhere in the tropical zone [...] an extraordinarily developed race of anthropomorphised monkeys" (ENGELS, 2010, p. 01).

Regardless of the era, labour moves the material world and the world of ideas. As well as being material, the importance of work is also ideological. Labels are established for each person, because the system of recognition generated as a method of ennobling workers is based on them producing satisfactorily. However, this is sometimes done in an alienated way, since many workers have no idea of the profit they make for the owners of the goods of production. In this sense, Marx (1989) explains that in the capitalist mode of production:

> The labourer becomes poorer the more wealth he produces, the more his production increases in power and extent. The labourer becomes a cheaper commodity the more goods he produces. [...] labour doesn't just produce commodities; it also produces itself and the worker as a commodity, and precisely in the same proportion as it produces goods. (p.159).

In some professions, the result of the work is concrete and tangible, capable of being evaluated objectively and precisely. In the case of teachers, this process is much more complex, since the work of art is not tangible and concrete, because the process of educating the student or the commodity formed cannot be clearly measured, it is subjective.

However, this fact does not prevent us from drawing up some parameters on the subject. Historically, Physical Education has served the interests of groups and as their interests change, so do the objectives of the professional's work. Physical education appeared linked to eugenic ideals of regeneration and whitening of the race (SOARES, 2007, p.18), hygienist ideals, character development, obedience and respect for the country. However, the outstanding characteristic that has not changed significantly is the political and critical training of these professionals.

The teaching profession has been discouraging the group of teachers who work in schools. Whether it's because students are more rebellious and disinterested, or because of poor working conditions and low salaries. According to data from SINPRO in Rio Grande do Sul, poor working conditions combined with low pay lead many teachers to leave the profession. In 2008, 36 per cent of contract terminations were resignations. In 2010, the rate rose to 45 per cent. This reality reflects the quality and neglect of training. Also according to SINPRO Rio Grande do Sul, between May 2008 and August 2009, "[...] 49% of the teachers interviewed were undergoing treatment with medication and other procedures. 45 per cent said they had experienced some kind of work-related physical or mental health problem." (p. 8). 78% reported frequent tiredness and exhaustion in the last 6 months. 20% of these professionals use antidepressant medication (AVANSINI, 2011, p. 8).

The lack of politicisation or the small possibility of improvements and progress discourage the group. There is a lack of tools for the struggle, for the class struggle, which appears mischaracterised and is often difficult to recognise, let alone transform the current order. You can't change practice without knowing it. In this process, the teacher assumes the role of the dominated in the face of a dominant, bourgeois group.

The lack of knowledge and tools favours the transformation of education into marketing, into merchandise, and also favours the alienation of professionals. Within this problem, labour is a producer of commodities and it is in this process that human beings become brutalised, because it is not possible to be human and intelligible, not in such adverse working conditions. It's enough to carry out predetermined actions in the shortest possible time.

> [...] labour is external to the worker, that is, it doesn't belong to his nature [...] therefore, the worker only feels himself outside of work, while in work he feels himself outside of himself. Thus, his work is not voluntary, but imposed, forced labour. It is not the fulfilment of a need, but merely a means of satisfying other needs. [...] the exteriority of labour for the worker is apparent in the fact that it doesn't belong to him, that in work he doesn't belong to himself, but to someone else. [...] he belongs to another and is the loss of himself (MARX, 1989, p.162).

Alienation because the professional's time and health are compromised, they don't have their basic needs met and they have to work hard to overcome these shortcomings. And, in fact, few find the breath to study, fight and emancipate themselves. Despite being necessary and urgent, we know that this is a tiring and exhausting process.

I consider the act of alienation of human activity, labour, in two ways: the relation of the worker to the product of labour as to a foreign object that dominates him; and the relation of labour to the act of production within labour. "[...] this is self-alienation, as opposed to the aforementioned alienation from the thing" (MARX, 1989, p.163).

In Taffarel (1993), specifically in topic *2.1 The labour process,* it was pointed out that existence is made through work, which is made possible by contact with nature, which with the advent of techniques makes it possible to accumulate goods, exchange and consequently surplus value, this process favours fetishism. The author also points to the specialisation and division of labour, which makes it possible to recognise:

> [...] the culmination of this process in the separation between free labour and the objective conditions of its realisation; in the separation between the means of labour and the object of labour; in the separation of the worker from the labour process, reducing him to simple labour-power; in the total separation between use, exchange and accumulation; in the separation between industrial, commercial and agricultural labour; in the separation between town and country; in the separation between designing and executing, in short, in the separation between theory and practice (TAFFAREL, 1993, p. 57).

This movement favours the alienation of workers and their disqualification, which is established by capital and increases "the real subordination of labour to capital" (TAFFAREL, 1993, p. 63). The problem is that this system doesn't work as well as it used to; in fact, it's in crisis (TAFFAREL, 1993).

Although there are many teachers who are resigned and uninterested in change, their class is on the brink. In this way, I think the government will have to release some benefit so that they don't decide to unite against the system. As Marx (1974) pointed out, a united class is very strong and the lack of control of groups can lead to violent actions, revolution and even the search for an egalitarian society.

Capital - still on the ideological question - under the premise of work as an obligation for all, incorporates the idea of work as a fundamental right. A right that is more formal than real, since the market doesn't cater for all workers, just as quality education doesn't cater for everyone.

With the crises of capitalism and rising unemployment, there are growing social problems, evident in all spheres: health, education, leisure and culture. There are many people dying of hunger and thirst, without basic hygiene conditions, without access to formal education, let alone a quality one, without possibilities or conditions to practise leisure and culture. In short, there is a large population that is alien to all social development.

The reality is crueler. Not only are people excluded from the benefits of development, they are also stigmatised. There is an ideological issue at play that attributes to the unfortunate and unemployed a conception that they are complacent, unintelligent or uninterested.

In the final analysis, don't these conceptions and policies conceal a deep ideological violence in which the idea that the bourgeois state and the 'businessmen' and their collective intellectuals have done their duty by offering schools of total quality? Those who can't find work or are thrown out of the market do so because of incompetence or because they didn't make the right choices. In other words, the victims of the exclusionary system become their own executioners (FRIGOTTO, 2008, p. 46).

The discourse has changed and starts to consider men as essentially different, and this difference must be respected. So there are those who are more capable and those who are less capable; there are those who learn more slowly; there are those who are interested in this and those who are interested in that (SAVIANI, 2003, p.38-41).

Implicit in this is the ideological proposal of social mobility, which aims to introduce the fiction of the provisional nature of the social structure in the face of the reality of the global reproduction of classes in themselves. The widespread dissemination of some individual cases of spectacular social ascension helps to reinforce the fallacious argument that through personal effort, through the intensity of labour, anyone can gain access to the highest social scale. This model of ideology is not the result of a strategy that is linearly constructed and autonomously applied (PALENZUELA, 1995) by the media either.

Few are aware of this ideological issue and how it is constructed historically. The market conditions imposed by the interests of capital make it extremely difficult for classes to rise. Unemployment and the precariousness of work are elements that make better living conditions impossible. Since the labour market doesn't cater for everyone and considering that the jobs that offer decent working conditions and pay are limited. There are many disputes over a stable job. This favours individualism, competition and disregard for others. Characteristics of the capitalist mode of production.

Thus, with the division of labour there is a contradiction between the interest of each individual or family and the community interest of all the individuals who exchange with each other. As far as the division of labour is concerned, we know that as long as there is a split between private and common interests, and as long as activity is not divided voluntarily but naturally, man's action itself becomes an alienated and opposing power for him, which subjugates him instead of him dominating it. As soon as labour begins to be distributed, each man has a specific and exclusive circle of activity imposed on him, which he cannot leave and must continue to leave if he doesn't want to lose his means of subsistence - whereas in communist society each man does not have an exclusive circle of activity. The power of production, the state, society and consciousness can and must contradict each other, because the division of labour makes it possible for spiritual activity and material activity, enjoyment and work, production and consumption to be carried out by different individuals (MARX and ENGELS, 2009, p. 46). The capitalist mode of production exposes its limits because:

> The current economic crisis shows that the neoliberal policy has not been able to recover and develop capitalism: it has abolished control over financial flows and created the conditions for uncontrolled speculation, with serious damage to the production process; it has increased the state

> apparatus, although it has reduced the state's social activity, which has been transferred to the private sector, and it has accentuated social inequalities and the concentration of wealth. The social consequences of this policy coincide with a reality of unemployment and misery of overwhelming proportions among workers all over the world, aggravated by the flexibility of labour and the perversity of the system of fixed-term contracts. These objective conditions, with their new specificities, exacerbate social contradictions, plus the crisis in political relations and the fading of moral values in a context in which social bonds are dissolving, making it possible to speak of a crisis of civilisation (SCHLESENER, 2010, p. 72).

The most crucial dimension of the limits of capital and capitalist development at the end of this century is the destruction of jobs - structural unemployment syndrome - job insecurity (flexibilisation), linked to the abolition of the hard-won social rights of the working class, especially and more broadly in around 20 countries. This process is due to the combination of exclusionary globalisation, which increases unequal development, and the private monopoly of science and technology (FRIGOTTO, 2008, p. 41).

> There are currently around 38 million unemployed people in rich countries alone. According to the ILO, approximately 30% of the economically active population, i.e. people who are able to work, are thrown into unemployment or, at best, into precarious work (FRIGOTTO, 2008, p. 27).

In Brazil alone, of the 78 billion that make up the economically active population, it is estimated that 60 per cent are in the informal sector. Fifteen years ago, the scenario was the opposite (ANTUNES, 2004 cited by SANTOS JUNIOR, 2005, p.33).

On the other hand, history shows that workers have maintained a certain level of resistance to the pretensions of capital and that their identification with the company's objectives has not been as complete as their bosses had hoped (BRAVERMAN, 1975 cited by PALENZUELA, 1995).

It is possible to identify some degree of convergence between some of these new forms of work organisation and management and the historical demands of workers' movements, in their resistance to coercive disciplinary methods and their struggle for a humanisation of work. However, the more "virtuous" looking practices have not had the diffusion that some analysts predicted in the 1970s and 1980s and coexist with clear signs of increased pressure on workers' performance, which often takes the form of demanding compulsory commitment or consent to business objectives. From the 1990s onwards, especially, mass unemployment seems to have greatly intensified the potential for subjection of workers who are employed, either through heteronomous imposition or through the introjection of employer goals and values (CATTANI and HOLZMANN, 2006).

Faced with the impositions of capital and its hegemonic power, we have to:

> At a certain stage of development, the material productive forces of society come into contradiction with the existing relations of production or, what is their legal expression, with the property relations within which they have moved until then. From being forms of development of the productive forces, these relations become their obstacle (MARX, 1977, p.25).

Explaining the contradictions between productive forces and relations of production is an objective of Marxism, as is understanding how they work and seeking to revolutionise reality with a view to a more egalitarian society. This is because the relations of production have been painful for the vast majority who do not have access to the minimum conditions of dignity. After all, we can't say that capitalism is a success in a world where 3 billion out of a total of 5.7 billion inhabitants live on less than 2 dollars a day (FRIGOTTO, 2008). We are part of a system that condemns % of the world's population to living on 1 dollar a day and that exploits 300 million children in the labour market (SANTOS JUNIOR, 2005).

Bearing in mind the category of dialectics, totality and contradiction, we understand that the current mode of production is running out of steam and a new model is needed, because nature will not bear such exploitation, just as the mass of workers will not bear their burden and will become indignant towards revolution.

Faced with these problems and contradictions caused by the social division of labour, the materialist-historical and dialectical framework aims to overcome the injustices of a class dispossessed of knowledge, culture and art, which the bourgeoisie has appropriated. Marx and Engels (2009) point out that the communist revolution is directed against the mode of activity to this day, eliminates alienated labour and overcomes the domination of all classes by suppressing the classes themselves. It is the expression of the dissolution of all classes and nationalities into the heart of today's society. For both the mass production of this communist consciousness and the realisation of the cause itself, a massive transformation of men is needed, which can only take place in a practical movement, in a revolution.

Links between the Mode of Production, Labour and Education

As mentioned, the current mode of production does not correspond to the interests of the majority who have their rights stolen by a class that has historically manipulated reality and ideologies in order to justify its hegemony. In order to overcome this issue, it is urgent to better understand what the mode of production is, as well as its relations.

Thus, the mode of production is the category in the work of Marx and Engels that expresses the totality of relations in which human practices are inscribed, being, at the same time, an expression that carries the particular (labour as a vital human activity) and the universal (society, the contradictory and dialectical social relations that men establish between themselves in the historical process of carrying out the work of producing existence)[2] .

Whenever the productive forces undergo a transformation, so does professional training and the consequent production of knowledge about this training, which is surrounded by a class struggle. There is a relationship between these mechanisms, and a change in one of them implies a reorganisation of the whole. In this movement, there is the class struggle in which the bourgeoisie fights to remain in control and the masses try to conquer their rights and ascend socially.

This whole mechanism is a consequence of changing social needs and the urgency of adapting training to the realm of needs. So the concrete interferes with the ideological and not the other way round, as Hegel pointed out. Production changes in order to solve the problems posed by materiality and there is a dialectical relationship between the two. When the productive forces advance, there is a reduction in the time needed to produce more productive force with less time needed for the production of life, so that there is more free time (for a select class) for the production of knowledge.

In other words, historically the freeing up of labour would make it possible to increase dedication to learning, but this is not the case for the majority. Capital exploits the proletariat so that the bourgeoisie have access to everything that the productive forces have made possible, in other words, consumer goods, technology and access to the basic necessities of life. The obstacle lies in the existence of private property and productive forces (land, man, tools, techniques). Thus, labour power is the property of the bourgeois.

Therefore, the advance of the productive forces benefits a small group that owns the production of existence and if human existence is not guaranteed by nature, it is not a natural gift, it has to be produced by men themselves, being the product of labour, this means that man is not born a man. He becomes a man and is not born knowing how to produce himself as such. He needs to learn how to be a man, he needs to learn how to produce his own existence. Therefore, the production of man is, at the same time, his formation, in other words, an educational process. In such a way that the origin of education coincides with the origin of man himself (SAVIANI, 2007).

---

[2] Conceptual definition made by Elza Margarida de Mendonça Peixoto in the subject Leisure offered at the State University of Londrina on 4th May 2010.

From the outset, the relationship between labour and education is one of identity. Men learnt to produce their existence in the very act of producing it. They learnt to work by working. By dealing with nature and relating to each other, men educated themselves and new generations. The production of existence implies the development of forms and contents whose validity is established by experience, which constitutes a real learning process. On communal property, education was identified with life. These are the historical-ontological foundations of the labour-education relationship. Historical foundations because they refer to a process produced and developed over time by the actions of men themselves. Ontological foundations because the product of this action, the result of this process, is the very being of men (SAVIANI, 2007).

As the social division of labour becomes more complex, so does training for work. The production of knowledge about training is a consequence of this process of complexification (VÁSQUEZ, 1977). Training has to do with the historical struggle of the working class, it has to do with capital, capitalism and the class struggle, in short, with the struggle for workers' rights. However, ideological instruments are created about the school's potential to train 'human capital'.

There is a dense body of literature dealing with the limits of (industrial) development centred on the Taylorist/Fordist or post-Fordist perspective and the acute crisis of capital expansion, job insecurity and structural unemployment, which, in our opinion, allows us to learn the theoretical-empirical axis that allows us to advance and tension both studies in the area, and, above all, the conceptions and policies of basic education, technical-vocational training and qualification, requalification and retraining processes on the agenda in the 1990s in Brazil, marked by a productivist perspective. This perspective reiterates, apparently with new concepts and categories, the economistic vision of human capital theory and has the World Bank and the hegemonic apparatuses of businessmen as its collective intellectuals (FRIGOTTO, 2008, p. 36). It is always understood that this policy is still aimed at productivity today.

> Investment in 'human capital' became the golden key to solving the riddle of underdevelopment and international, regional and individual inequalities. The theory of human capital went through an intense internal debate, particularly in the 1960s and 1970s, and at the same time was widely used politically and ideologically in the definition of educational macro-policies guided by international and regional organisations. In Brazil, during the period of the military dictatorship, as Saviani (1988) shows, two reforms - university reform in 1968 and primary and secondary education reform in 1971 - structured the education system within technicist and economist parameters, inspired by this theoretical-ideological formulation (FRIGOTTO, 2008, p. 37 and 38).

The balance sheet of recent history, of the violent way in which capital resolves its crises to maximise profit rates, leaves no doubt that in fact the ideology of human capital, as a strategy for reducing international, regional and individual inequalities, apprehends social relations in a skewed way and distorts the structural reasons for exclusion (FRIGOTTO, 2008, p. 44).

In this way, it can be seen that the entire mechanism of the current mode of production revolves around the best way to produce surplus value and this is made possible by the commodity, an element that produces use-value and can have exchange-value. Thus, the accumulation of commodities and their exchange or sale leads the capitalist to profit (MARX, 2008). The wealth of capitalist societies is based on the immense accumulation of commodities, and the commodity in isolation is the elementary/basic form of this wealth (MARX, 1989). The aim is therefore to turn everything into a commodity, even property that cannot be materialised, regardless of the moral or ethical value attributed to it.

With this commodification movement in mind, education has a price and it costs a lot. In line with the ideals of capitalism and the market, education is geared towards rapid training in line with the precepts of industrialisation: rapidly formed goods of dubious quality that aim to meet the primary needs of the market, in which the worker has no capacity for broad and in-depth reflection on the value of their work. They know little about the basic concepts and objectives of the field, so they can't justify the social importance of their work. This is due to disorganised training.

In order to create merchandise, it is necessary not only to produce use-value, but to produce it for others, to give rise to social use-value (MARX, 2006, p.57-68). And it's in this movement that training fits in, as it creates high-value commodities for society that can generate greater accumulated value. "The commodity is first and foremost an external object, a thing which, by its properties, satisfies human needs, whatever their nature, whatever their origin, whether they come from the stomach or from fantasy" (MARX, 2006, p.57).

The usefulness of a thing makes it a use-value. But this utility is not something aerial, as it is determined by the material properties inherent in the commodity and only exists through it. Use-values constitute the material content of wealth (MARX, 2006, p. 57-68).

It can be said that education is a cheap commodity governed by capital. And under the public apparatus, we see a movement by the state to disengage from its obligation towards education. This means that, on the other hand, we need to fight more and more for a quality, public and secular education that enables students to read the historical, economic and social context in which they are involved.

It can be seen that the market is at the centre of training issues (MOREIRA, 2007; SANTOS JUNIOR, 2005). However, this training should focus on the acquisition and maintenance of knowledge that is historically relevant to society and should be everyone's right, as Saviani (2008) pointed out.

There is the fallacious argument that education works badly because it is not linked to the needs of the labour market. To accept this argument is to accept that education must train for competition in a labour market that is increasingly shrinking due to neoliberal policy itself, which disseminates the idea that education must adapt to market demands, which are many and change extremely quickly. This same market directs education from the neoliberal perspective, which is exclusionary and unequal (GENTILI, 1996 apud ANDERÁOS, 2005).

At root, we need to question the analyses that seek to adjust education and vocational training to productive restructuring seen as a consequence of the new technical base and globalisation processes. This perspective is based on a vision of development, science and technology that is alien to social relations and based on the assumption of full employment. To what extent do our insistence on the impact of new technologies on the world of production and work, without understanding them themselves as a product of exclusionary social relations, not make our analyses limited and adaptive? (FRIGOTTO, 2008).

It is necessary to transpose the project of society into schools, into Higher Education Institutions, because these institutions are interfering and being interfered with by the totality. It is necessary to analyse the organisation of pedagogical work based on significant and relevant issues, such as the definition of "an alternative historical project, the democratisation of power relations, the collective configuration of a political-pedagogical project that involves collective work, methodological unity, student self-organisation and living work, as the founding and organising axis of the curriculum" (TAFFAREL, 1993, p. 103).

In this sense, Taffarel (1993) adds that studies from a Marxist perspective on the relationship between education and society emphasise the role of the capitalist school in producing individuals who serve the economic sector of society, equipping them with an appropriate subjectivity (personality traits, attitudes, ideological inclinations); distributing a certain amount and an appropriate type of knowledge among the social classes, which contributes to social division and reproduction.

The category of education is among the first-order determinations that characterise humanity. However, like other categories, such as the family, language or social organisation, within the capitalist system, education has been subordinated to the logic of capital and its operating imperatives. The phenomenon of education is thus converted into a double dimension: on the one hand, we have a fetishised or alienating education and, on the other, a commodity that, in the form of a service (and therefore no longer a human right), is subject to the laws and forces of the market. It's important to note that when the latter happens, capital-dominated education becomes a second-order determination within the social metabolism of capital. This is where identities or institutions such as schools, universities, research centres and the mass media are constituted[3] .

It is well known that the integration and adjustment of "undeveloped" or "developing" countries to the process of globalisation and productive restructuring, under a new scientific and technological base, depends on basic education, vocational training, qualification and retraining. But not just any education and training. So what is this education and training? Education and training that develops basic skills in terms of knowledge, attitudes and values, producing competences for quality management, productivity and competitiveness and, consequently, employability. All these parameters must be defined in the world of production and, therefore, the reliable collective intellectuals of this new conformism are international organisations (World Bank, ILO) and organisations linked to the world of production in each country (FRIGOTTO, 2008).

> The proposals for basic education and technical-vocational training, under the ideology of skills and competences for employability, re-qualification and retraining, as they stand today, disconnected from a democratic and public proposal for development that integrates an economic, political and cultural project with a clear generation of jobs and income, or, for those who are fighting for a new type of social relations (socialist), are dominantly reduced to an ideological wrapping (FRIGOTTO, 2008, p. 49).

After all, what is the point of the idea of education and training for

---

[3] Translation by the author. "We place the category of education among the first-order determinations that characterise humanity. However, like other categories, such as the family, language or social organisation, within the capitalist system, education is becoming subordinate to the logic of capital and its operating imperatives. In such a way that this system converts education, as a social and human category in general, into a dimension subsumed to the logic of capital and its valorisation, while at the same time expressing the formal function that every "individual" supposedly has to possess in order to "live" and reproduce in society. The educational phenomenon is thus converted into a double dimension: on the one hand, we have a fetishised or enjambed education and, on the other, a commodity which, in the form of a service (and no longer a human right), is subject to the laws and forces of the market as such. It is important to emphasise that when the latter happens, capital-dominated education becomes a second-order determination within the social metabolism of capital. This is where entities or institutions such as schools, universities, research centres and mass media come into play." (VALENCIA, 2010, p. 23).

employability, retraining and professional reconversion, within an endemic reality of structural unemployment, mass superfluous labour and the empirical evidence that shows that today, through the incorporation of technology, there is an increase in productivity and economic growth without an increase in the level of employment? (FRIGOTTO, 2008, p. 46).

Unfortunately, in most cases, Physical Education professionals graduate unemployed and remain so for a long time. Until they turn to public tenders, discouraged by the market, or subject themselves to precarious working conditions, often working informally, without a decent salary.

Flexible accumulation brings with it a discourse of overcoming structural duality through education and knowledge, in the sense of demanding that workers incorporate competences to carry out different work activities with more sophisticated degrees of complexity. However, the limits of this discourse are pointed out to us, given that the structural duality, for the author, will only be overcome if the contradiction between the ownership of the means of production and the labour force is overcome (KUENZER, 2007) and the Physical Education professional is part of this process. Around the 1990s, this professional's value was diminished by the neoliberal project. In recent years, as part of the third way neoliberal proposals, Pereira (2009) observes that Physical Education has been expanding its participation in the education project for a renewed bourgeois sociability and in this movement, Higher Education Institutions in the area of Physical Education have tried to offer a course that would satisfy students and "make it possible to act broadly in the labour market and not, quality professional preparation, to meet the needs of society". (ANDERÁOS, 2005, p. 163).

This objective contributes to the weakening of the theoretical training of Physical Education professionals as a result of curricular restructuring processes that do not take into account the organisation of the pedagogical work process and the production and appropriation of knowledge. These reformulations aim to provide qualifications for certain specialised tasks and functions, established by the labour market - specific functions to be performed in specific situations according to the Taylorist model (TAFFAREL, 1993).

The training of this professional has been predominantly alienated, since it enables a higher education professional to exercise a given profession through the appropriation of knowledge that is given as finished, fragmented and specialised, restricting the possibility of overcoming the mechanisms of alienation in academic training (TAFFAREL, 1993, p. 208). With regard to undergraduate programmes in general, the author highlights a series of problems:

[...] the disconnection between the training process in undergraduate courses and primary and secondary education; the dichotomy between theory and practice; the lack of knowledge production and systematic research in the courses; the segregation of knowledge; the fragmentation and division of areas of knowledge; the dichotomy between undergraduate and graduate programmes; institutional factors hindering the improvement of the courses (TAFFAREL, 1993, p. 103).

The purpose of this work was to explain what the production of knowledge on training is and how it is produced. My aim was to survey, catalogue, compile and analyse the production of knowledge relating to studies on Physical Education training, with the aim of recognising: (1) the flow and volume of this production over time in order to know when it began in Brazil; (2) the main authors who are producing in this area in Brazil and the main references and theoretical frameworks adopted in the theses; (3) the major debates and themes that are privileged and motivate this production. It is therefore a question of recognising this production by mapping the concerns that motivate it and the debates from which it multiplies.

Thanks to the analyses carried out, I found that, in terms of the flow and volume of dissertations and theses produced, production began in 1982 with one paper, and the following year the same. Subsequently, production came to a standstill and resumed in 1988. Since then, production has been inconsistent and, after 1998, it has grown significantly. In 2009, there was a slight increase to 9 works, certainly due to the increase in postgraduate programmes and incentives from funding bodies. In this way, I have identified a fairly recent and inconstant production.

I noticed that in the 1980s researchers were interested in discussing issues relating to critical training, the legislation that guides training, teaching practice, competences for professional practice, the liberal trend in professional training and school physical education. There was almost a consensus that professional competences would solve the problems of practice.

The early 1990s, on the other hand, were marked by productions that focused on the discussion of pedagogical work; dealing with knowledge; the subjects of recreation and leisure in the training curriculum; human motricity at Unicamp; the relationship between intention and the pedagogical action of undergraduates; assessment during training; folklore and popular culture; citizenship in the Physical Education course in higher education; training and intervention in Physical Education; science and professional training; self-perception of competence; the subject of basketball in training; proposals for professional training; occupation of the labour market; disintegrated training and, finally, the historical emancipatory possibilities in the labour market. As a result, I realised that the subject under investigation has changed and the number of articles has increased significantly.

I would point out that during the 1980s and 1990s, the number of studies on regulation and knowledge production was very low, which reinforced my premise that a lot is produced on vocational training, but little is studied and known about the profile of this production.

Of all the dissertations and theses found in higher education institutions, UNICAMP is the most productive with a total of 23 works, and is a reference for the study of professional training in Physical Education in Brazil. This is followed by UFSC with 19 works; UFSM with 9 works; UFBA with 5 works; USP, PUC-SP and UFRGS with 4 works each; UFRJ, UFPE and UNESP/RC with 3 works each. These institutions are a reference point for those who want to enter postgraduate programmes or want to find out more about the work on this subject.

I identified that a large proportion of the papers focused on the training of PE teachers, a smaller proportion focused on the training of PE professionals, and a few did not make it clear whether they were referring to teachers or professionals. I therefore noticed a greater gap in the production of knowledge about professionals than about teachers. As opportunities for working in the non-school labour market increase, the number of studies is growing.

The themes found during the analyses that motivated the production were: assessment (11); curriculum (9); history (7); intervention (5); policies (8); training processes (19); knowledge production (12); regulation (1) and knowledge and competences (15); theories, conceptions and methodologies (1). There has been a lot of research into the following themes: training processes; knowledge and competences; and theories, conceptions and methodologies. These are more technical aspects of education and teaching. The themes of history and politics have received little attention, which certainly jeopardises the quality of the output.

As for the supervisors, I found that Tojal was the most productive with a total of 7 works (3 theses and 4 dissertations), followed by Nascimento with 5 dissertations; Gallardo (2 theses and 2 dissertations); Krug with 4 dissertations and Neto with 3 dissertations. This implies seeing them as a reference, as opinion formers who propagate their theoretical framework and their conception of vocational training. Freitas, Hunger, Kunz, Leiro, Mahoney, Shigunov and Vaz all had 2 dissertations.

It is essential to know the ideology that surrounds these counsellors in order to know which ideology influences the production of knowledge in Brazil. In a forthcoming study, I intend to analyse the work of João Batista Andreotti Gomes Tojal, Celi Nelza Zulke Taffarel, Samuel de Souza Neto and Hugo Norberto Krug. The intended expositions will consider: (a) the physical and structural description (pre-textual, textual and post-textual elements); (b) the justifications presented by the authors for the need to study, research and work in the area of training in education, as well as the historical context that explains their production.

I presented the historical context that explains this production, which is that of a capitalist society that seeks to extract surplus value even if it sacrifices nature, education, customs and morals. It is the era of politicking, politics in the pejorative sense, which takes place through exchanges of favours and interests between the powerful or their aspirants, in which education is no exception, tied to the interests of the market and surrounded by a neoliberal policy that favours segregation and the loss of class consciousness.

The production of knowledge, in this context, is seen as the great productive force of the 21st century, as it enables greater accumulation of capital. As a commodity, it acts for capital as a means of production in professional training and interventions, influenced by the interests of the bourgeoisie, such as positivism itself, which values empiricist and quantitative methods.

These methods have favoured an era of fragmentation, in which everything is subject to fragmentation. Society is divided into classes, higher education institutions are divided into departments, education is shattered, thinking is fragmented and there is no construction of the whole, there are only the pieces of the puzzle, the society of specialists.

I've identified that every division that is put in place is in the interests of capitalists, a divided society that is easily manipulated, becoming competitive and individualistic and; when a sector is about to explode, about to make a real demonstration, the system allows some perks such as salary increases and reduced working hours. In this way, demonstrations are softened and order is maintained. This is when we expect and need a more cohesive society, one that is more attentive to others, their rights and needs, and integrated higher education institutions in which knowledge is produced at a macro level, with broad training.

This time has long-standing problems that are not restricted to Physical Education, but to many fields of endeavour. The separation between theory and practice, the positivist attitude towards training, the difference in training conditions for courses, which is increasingly lightened, the fever for distance learning, teachers in precarious working conditions who don't change their professional practice, outdated course curricula that are often stuck on novelties, young students who create unrealistic expectations of the course, who have poor previous training and are quickly disinterested in the course, in short, these are all factors that lead to poor professional training.

Within Physical Education we can see a biological vision of society, which serves the interests of capital without being aware of it. The field has pointed out, and still points out, the issues of order, moral uprightness, making the subject responsible for their health, physique, safety, training and salary. These are some of the consequences of the mode of production that the population has chosen.

I have shown that higher education institutions are not training competent professionals to work in the labour market. This is because training policies are increasingly rooted in the capitalist mode of production, geared towards accelerated, cheaper and, consequently, lower quality training. These professionals are trained from the same perspective as commodities, in which the principles of the liberalist market prioritise freeing up the basic functions of the state.

The university does not train in the breadth of the arts, science and technology. It trains for specific areas of activity, an uncritical and alienated education. Depending on the course, alienation and distance from reality can be even greater. The context is one of training full of contradictions, professional disqualification and disregard for training.

The system of scientific production doesn't reach the teachers in the network and, in general, there is no interest in the majority knowing about the system that oppresses them. They deal with reformism, often based on liberalist principles, but they don't go any further, they don't deal with revolution, with the possibility of a more egalitarian society. In this production there is a preoccupation with specificities, there is a clear division between sub-areas and the notion of the whole is lost, so specialists are formed who know so much from so little.

Bibliography

AVANSINI, Carolina. Lack of structure makes education precarious. *Folha de Londrina*. Londrina, 2011, p. 1-8.

Available at :
www.capes.gov.br/images/stories/download/avaliacao/EDU_FIS 15out2009.pdf, p. 01. Accessed on: 05 July 2010a.

Available at :
www.qualis.capes.gov.br/webqualis/consulta periodicos.faces. Accessed on: 21 August 2010b.

CATTANI, A. D. & HOLZMANN. *Dictionary of labour and technology.* Porto alegre: Editora da UFRGS, 2006.

COSTA, A. S. F.; CRUVIENL, A. F.; MACHADO J. C.;PINTO, K. C.; SACARDO, M. S.; SOUZA, J. A.; LIMA, L. F. Analysis of scientific production in journals on the subject of teacher training. Available at: *<http://www.sepq.org.br/IIsipeq/anais/pdf/poster4/04.pdf.>* Accessed on 12/07/2010.

ENGELS, Friedrich. *Origin of the Family, Private Property and the State.* Rio de Janeiro: Bertrand Brasil, 1995.

ENGELS, Friedrich; MARX, Karl. For the critique of political economy. Available at: *<http:* www.marxists.org/portugues/marx/1859/08/15.htm> Accessed on: 28 July 2009.

______. *The situation of the working class in England.* São Paulo: Boitempo, 2008.

______. On the role of labour in the transformation of ape into man. Available at: <http: www.marxists.org/portugues/marx/.../macaco.htm> Accessed on: 17 Feb. 2010.

FRIGOTTO, Gaudêncio. *Education and the crisis of real capitalism.* São Paulo: Cortez, 1995.

______. Education, the crisis of wage labour and development: theories in conflict. In: *Educação e crise do trabalho: perspectivas de final de século.*

Petrópolis, Vozes, 2008.

FRIGOTTO, Gaudêncio; NOSELLA, P.; GOMES, C. M.; ARRUDA, M.; ARROYO, M. *Trabalho e conhecimento: dilemmas na educação do trabalhador.* São Paulo: Cortez, 2004.

KUENZER, Acácia. *Secondary and vocational education: the policies of the neoliberal state.* São Paulo: Cortez, 2007.

KRUG, Hugo Norberto. *Participatory self-training network as a way of developing physical education professionals.* Thesis (Doctorate in Human Movement Science). 2004. Supervisor: Carmen Maria Andrade, UFSM, Santa Maria.

MARX, Karl. *Contribution to the Critique of Political Economy.* São Paulo: Martins Fontes, 1977.

______. *Economic and philosophical manuscripts and other texts.* São Paulo: Abril Cultural, 1978.

______. *Capital.* Rio de Janeiro: Brazilian Civilisation, 2008.

______. *Capital, Critique of Political Economy: The Process of the Production of Capital.* Translator: Reginaldo Sant'Anna. 24 ed. Rio de Janeiro: Civilização Brasileira, 2006.

______. For the critique of political economy. Available at: *http://www.marxists.org./portugues/marx/1859/prefacio.htm.* Accessed on: 28 July 2009.

______. *Economic-Philosophical Manuscripts.* São Paulo: Boitempo, 2009.

MARX, K.; ENGELS, F. *The German Ideology.* Portugal: Editorial Presença. Brazil: Livraria Martins Fontes, 1974.

______. *Critique of Education and Teaching.* Morares Publishing House, undated.

______. *Manifesto of the Communist Party.* S.P: Martin Claret, 2008.

______. *The German Ideology (Feuerbach).* São Paulo: Hucitec, 2009.

MOREIRA, Evando Carlos. *Contributions of stricto sensu postgraduate programmes to the training and performance of higher education teachers: the case of Physical Education.* 2007. Thesis (Doctorate in Physical Education), UNICAMP, Campinas.

PALENZUELA, Pablo. *The Cultures of Work: An Anthropological Approach.* Madrid, 1995.

PEIXOTO, Margarida de Mendonça. *Leisure studies in Brazil: appropriation of the work of Marx and Engels. 2007.* Thesis (Doctorate). Faculty of Education - State University of Campinas, Campinas.

______. Oral communication given at the course "Mode of Production, Labour and Education" at the State University of Londrina on 16 September 2010.

PEREIRA, Vinícius Costa. *Projects for physical education in times of productive restructuring.* 2009. Dissertation (Masters in Education). Fluminense Federal University, Niterói.

SANTOS JUNIOR, Cláudio de Lira. *The training of physical education teachers: the mediation of theoretical-methodological parameters.* 2005. Thesis (Doctorate in Education). UFBA, Salvador.

SAVIANI, Dermeval. *Escola e democracia: polêmicas do nosso tempo.* 36 ed. Campinas: Autores Associados, 2003.

______. Labour and education: ontological and historical foundations. *Revista Brasileira de Educação.* v.12 n.34. Rio de Janeiro Jan./Apr. 2007.

______. *Historical-critical pedagogy: first approaches.* 10 ed. Campinas: Autores Associados, 2008.

SCHLESENER, Anita Helena. Crisis and revolution: observations from the writings of Antonio Gramsci. *Germinal: Marxism and Education in Debate,* Londrina, v. 1, n. 2, p. 69-78; jan. 2010.

SEVERINO, Antônio Joaquim. *Methodology of scientific work.* São Paulo: Cortez, 2007.

SOARES, Carmen. *Physical Education: European roots and Brazil.* 4 ed.

Campinas: SP: Autores Associados, 2007.

TAFFAREL, Celi Nelza Zulke. *The training of Physical Education professionals: the pedagogical work process and dealing with knowledge in the Physical Education course.* 1993. Supervisor: Luis Carlos de Freitas. Thesis (Doctorate in Education), UNICAMP, Campinas.

VALENCIA, Adrain Sotelo. Crisis and revolution. *Germinal: Marxism and Education in Debate, Londrina,* v. 2, n. 1, p. 16-26; jan. 2010.

VÁSQUEZ, Adolfo Sánchez. *Philosophy of praxis.* Paz e Terra, 1977.

Table of contents

Printed by Books on Demand GmbH, Norderstedt / Germany